ARTSOURCE™
VOLUME 8
Stark Raving Clip Art

Created by Church Art Works™

ZondervanPublishingHouse
Grand Rapids, Michigan
A Division of HarperCollinsPublishers

ArtSource Volume 8: Stark Raving Clip Art

Copyright 1997 by Church Art Works™

Youth Specialties Books, 1224 Greenfield Dr., El Cajon, CA 92021, are published by Zondervan Publishing House, 5300 Patterson Ave. S.E., Grand Rapids, MI 49530.

ISBN 0-310-21787-3

Created by Church Art Works™, 875 High St. NE, Salem, OR 97301.

Printed in the United States of America

99 00/ /4

T A B L E   O F
CONTENTS

Enter a new era of creativity
with ArtSource™ clip art on CD-ROM!

Youth workers have been demanding it, and now it's here—the ultimate in clip art and convenience. Volumes 1-7 of the best-selling ArtSource™ clip art with the flexibility of CD-ROM. For Mac, Windows, and DOS.* Easy to use and absurdly affordable.

On the ArtSource™ CD-ROM:
- *Volume 1—Fantastic Activities*
- *Volume 2—Borders, Symbols, Holidays, & Attention Getters*
- *Volume 3—Sports*
- *Volume 4—Phrases & Verses*
- *Volume 5—Amazing Oddities & Appalling Images*
- *Volume 6—Spiritual Topics*
- *Volume 7—Variety Pack*

Of course, you can get all these ArtSource™ volumes in book form, too.

*System requirements: *Any word processing, desktop publishing, or other program supporting TIFF graphics (such as Microsoft® Word, WordPerfect™, Quark Xpress™, Adobe Photoshop™, PageMaker®, and others). CD-ROM drive.*

ACKNOWLEDGMENTS

Thanks to the hundreds of youth ministers who have submitted ideas for these illustrations.   Thanks also to the artists who contributed to this book:

Dave Adamson	Dave Baker	Mike Bartlett
Tom Finley	Von Glitschka	"Tito" Moore
John Nissen	Michelle Seefeldt	Wanda Stutzman

Also, thanks to our support team at Church Art Works™:

Kelley Adamson	Bruce Bottorff	Sharon Bryson
Tony Dyck	Cindy Kuiken	Ellen Zarfas
Nelson Zarfas		

INTRODUCTION

We've designed ArtSource™ to be a quick and complete sourcebook for your youth program promotions. It contains art from Church Art Works' extensive files of ministry clip art, as well as from other contributing artists. This ArtSource™ volume contains borders, symbols, and a variety of wacked-out clips. Future volumes will supply new subjects as well as additional art for the subjects in this volume and previous volumes.

We want this book and others in the series to be a valuable, time-saving asset to your ministry. You can help us with ideas for more clip art by using the Brainstorm Form on page 93. When you submit your ideas to us, you keep the creativity flowing—which assists thousands of youth workers in attracting students to their Bible studies and events.

LET'S BE CREATIVE!

This volume of ArtSource™ clip art gives you the chance to pump more life into your promotions and create excitement in your group. Just follow these four easy steps:

1. CREATE AN EXCITING IDEA. Advance planning and scheduling of your youth group activities is essential. But don't stop there. Hold separate brainstorming sessions to allow time for creativity to blossom. Creative ideas don't come easily in a board-meeting format, so get away to neutral territory of some sort with a few crazy idea people. Call it a Creativity Retreat if you want. Let the clip art in this book inspire some new ideas, too. Once the ideas are on paper, save the sorting out and logistics for later—the dates, the costs, the division of labor, etc., can wait until you get back in your office. A Creativity Retreat (or whatever you call it) helps you break away from everyday pressures in order to birth fresh ideas.

2. CREATE AN EXCITING MESSAGE. When you prepare your promotional piece, think like a teenager. Don't be trapped into listing just time, date, and place. Take a look at the examples on pages 9-12.

BASIC STEPS IN PREPARING PRINTED MATERIALS

Helpful tools that will make your job easier are a pair of scissors, an x-acto (or craft) knife, a ruler, a light blue pencil (nonreproducing) for layout, rubber cement (or glue stick or wax, for adhesive), tape, a few black markers (with felt tips of various widths), a T-square, triangles, sheets of transfer lettering ("rub-on" type), a technical pen, and a drafting table or drawing board. All of these tools are available at an art or drafting store.

Photocopy or cut out pieces of art from this book for your project. You can reduce it or enlarge it on a photocopier. Choose art that fits your subject.

Plan your layout. Sketch (on a separate piece of paper) where you want art and where you want copy (headlines and details). See pages 9-12 for ideas.

Use felt-tip pens, a typewriter, or a desktop computer to set your type. Assemble this in combination with the clip art and paste it on a clean white sheet or card for your "master."

Copy the master to reproduce as many printed pieces as you need for your event. Copying can be done on your photocopier or at a print shop.

3. CREATE AN EXCITING LOOK. *Think beyond the typical flier or announcement. Teenagers love the unusual. So instead of aligning things in straight lines, for example, place them at different angles on the page. Or if you usually use small type, think BIG TYPE. If you tend to illustrate your message with a normal-looking teenager (whatever that is), use a hippopotamus instead!*

One way to avoid getting trapped into the same old layout procedure is to first lay out the clip art on a big blank sheet, then work the headlines and copy around the clip art. Let the design be as big as you want, as long as it's fun and has impact. Working copy around the clip art (instead of the traditional order of laying out copy first, then filling in the blanks with clip art) creates unusual, attention-getting shapes and column widths. Plus it's easier to lay out—not to mention more fun!

Or use the big sheet to roughly sketch out small layout options—two- or three-inch versions. Explore radically different layouts of the elements in your piece. For example, in one sketch the art may be huge and the type small; in another, the type may be huge and the art sized fairly small. You have many different options with the same piece of clip art—such as repeating it several times for a border effect.

4. CREATE AN EXCITING ATTITUDE. *After committing your plans to God, promoting your event is the first step toward contacting those you want to reach. Stretch yourself and strive for the very best. This new attitude will be reflected in your work. Others will sense your desire for creativity and professionalism, and the enthusiasm will spread. As more people become involved in the project, you'll also stretch them. The results? Excitement as your team begins to focus on a worthwhile goal!*

In the next few pages we've given you creative examples of ways to use clip art. Use these ideas to launch your own exciting promotional pieces. Have fun!

HOT TIP #1
CREATIVE IDEA STARTERS

Use the same methods that advertising agencies use. First, look through this book for an illustration that grabs your attention. Then, begin to brainstorm for a creative headline.

EXAMPLE
Buzzard Brainstorm
...Scavenger Hunt...Be there or you're Dead Meat...Pot Luck...Hey Dead-Head... Hey Buzzard Breath...etc.

EXAMPLE
Mongoose Brainstorm
...Check this out...Stand up for your faith...Be on the alert...Don't be a weasel...etc.

In the brainstorming process look for humor, shock value, or unique phrases that stick in your mind. Write down all the obvious ideas and phrases that relate to the illustration. At this point don't even try to decide if it's a good or bad idea. Gather input from several creative (or crazy) friends. Use the dictionary, thesaurus, or slang dictionary to find additional words and phrases. Also allow enough time for your subconscious to work by taking a break (day dreaming or sleep usually activates this creative process). The best headline will eventually rise to the top of the list.

The next step is to tie all the informational copy back to the headline. Look for plays on words, double meanings, and quirky phrases that enhance the word picture you're creating. On this page are several examples to give you some ideas.

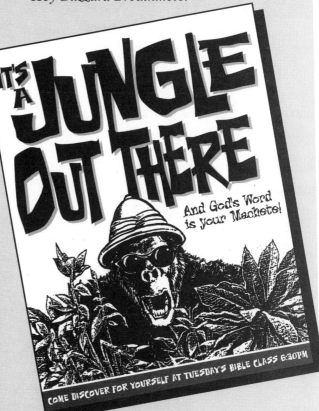

EXAMPLE
Gorilla Brainstorm
...The Great Adventure...It's a jungle out there...We've been looking 4U... Stop beating around the bush...etc.

HOT TIP #2

CREATIVE USE OF THE ART

Create unusual effects by enlarging and cropping the art. Fill a large portion of the page with the art, then fill the gaps with type. Be creative and change your design format occasionally to avoid looking the same all the tim

EXAMPLE
Coffee Dude
You don't have to use the entire clip-art image. Just enlarge and crop what you want.

(original art)

EXAMPLE
Freaky Face
Creatively cropped images help support your message.

ARE YOU A JESUS FREAK

Forsaking everything and following Christ is not an option. It is mandatory for a Christian. There is no room for lukewarm believers in the body of Christ.

(original art)

Combine several pieces of art to add a fun, wacky feel to your next publication. Remember–curiosity, humor, a shock value grab teenagers' attention. The more off-the-wall, the better!

EXAMPLE
Man & Frog
Combine two strange images and create an eye-catching layout.

Bring a Friend to church.

(original art)

EXAMPLE
Spark Plug
Create a concept based on any clip-art image you want.

IGNITE YOUR FAITH!

Read the Bible daily and give yourself a spiritual tune-up.

(original art)

HOT TIP #3
DON'T BE AFRAID TO REPEAT

You can repeat images by using random sizes or using identically sized art to create a pattern. Experimentation leads to creative solutions.

EXAMPLE
Alien Heads
Using clip art as a pattern can reinforce your concept.

EXAMPLE
Alien Heads
Using clip art at different sizes can give your layout depth and movement.

Overlap the different elements of your design for an interesting look. Cut out your art to leave a gap of white around some images to improve clarity in your visuals. For a thrasher-grunge look try copying several different type styles of your headline on top of one another and combine it with your illustration. Always check for readability so that your message won't be lost.

EXAMPLE
Engine Head
As you lay out type, don't be afraid to experiment. You'll be surprised by the result!

(white gap around art)

(white gap around art)

EXAMPLE
Engine Head
Let your type run off the page and be overlapped by your clip art.

11

HOT TIP #4

CONTINUITY IS THE KEY

By planning ahead you can add visual continuity to all your promotional materials for an event. Systematic, repeated use of the same art will increase credibility and build interest. Your next happening can look less like a mere activity and more like a Major Event. Face it–we live in a visually oriented society!

EXAMPLE
Music Dude
Select a visual that will be the most versatile for your particular needs.

(original Art)

(calendar)

(banner)

Choose a visual that fits the activity or event yo want to promote. Start advertising with your year or quarterly calendar. A video presentation, a larg eye-catching poster, or a giant banner 3-4 month prior to the event will introduce the graphic sty and begin to generate interest.

(ticket)

(Flier)

(brochure)

(button)

(poster)

Brochures, fliers, and handouts should be miniature versions of the poster. As you get closer to the event, T-shirts, tickets, and buttons can raise the anticipation levels. Promote your event with video presentations, notebook covers, backdrops, signage, etc. The possibilities are endless.

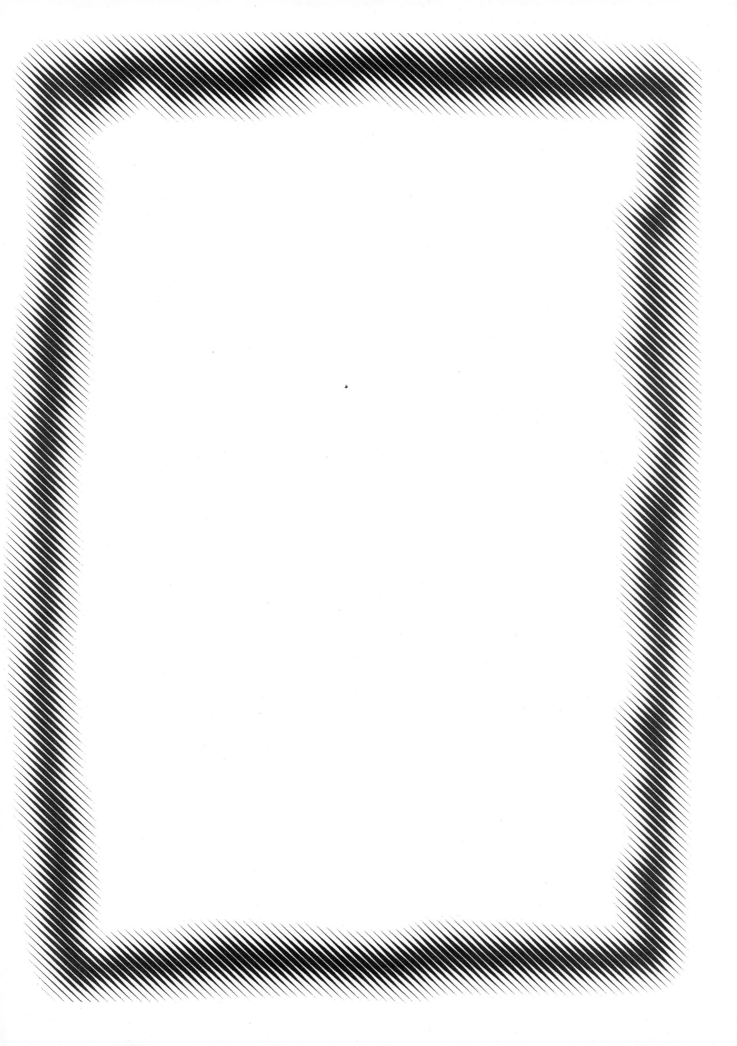

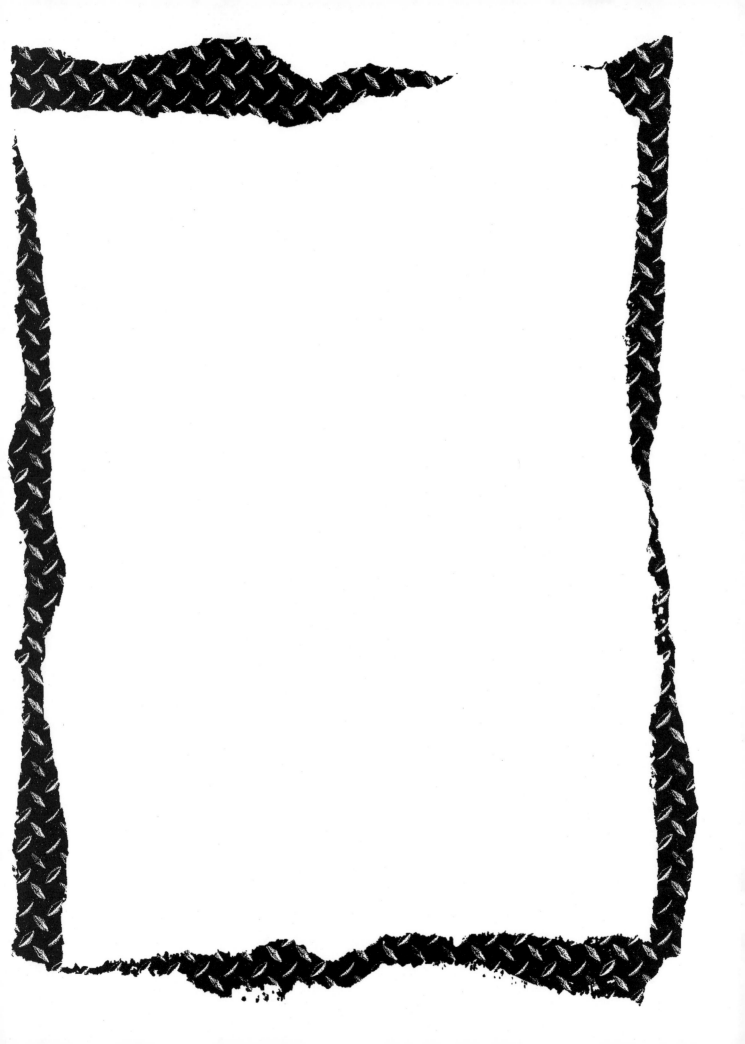

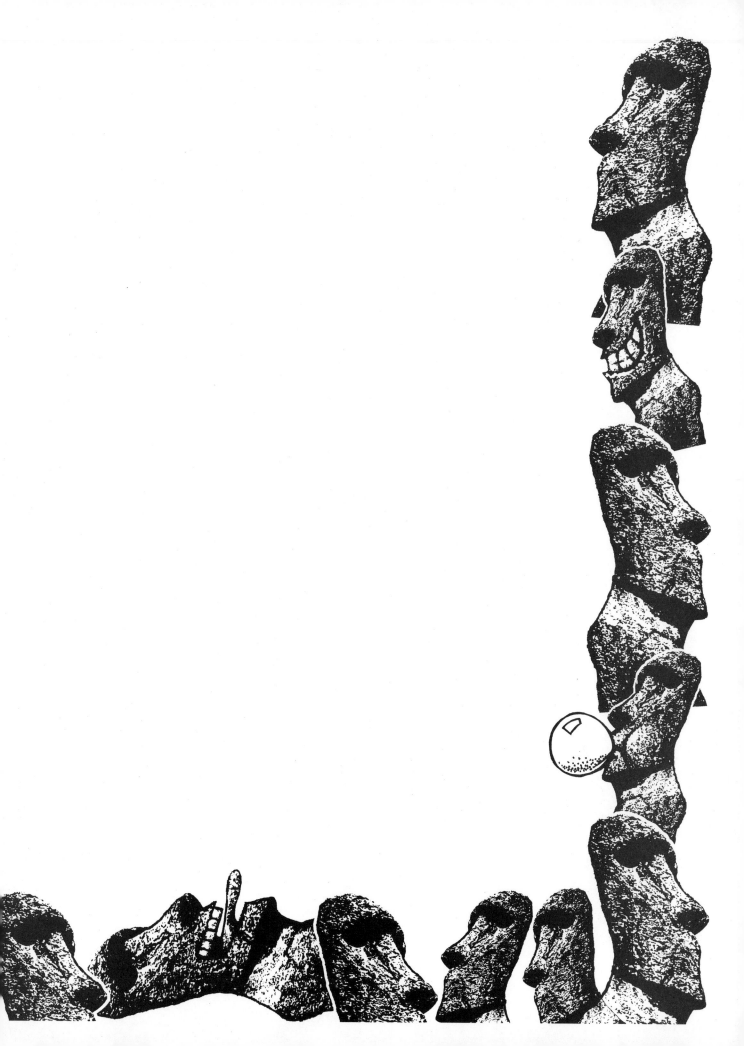

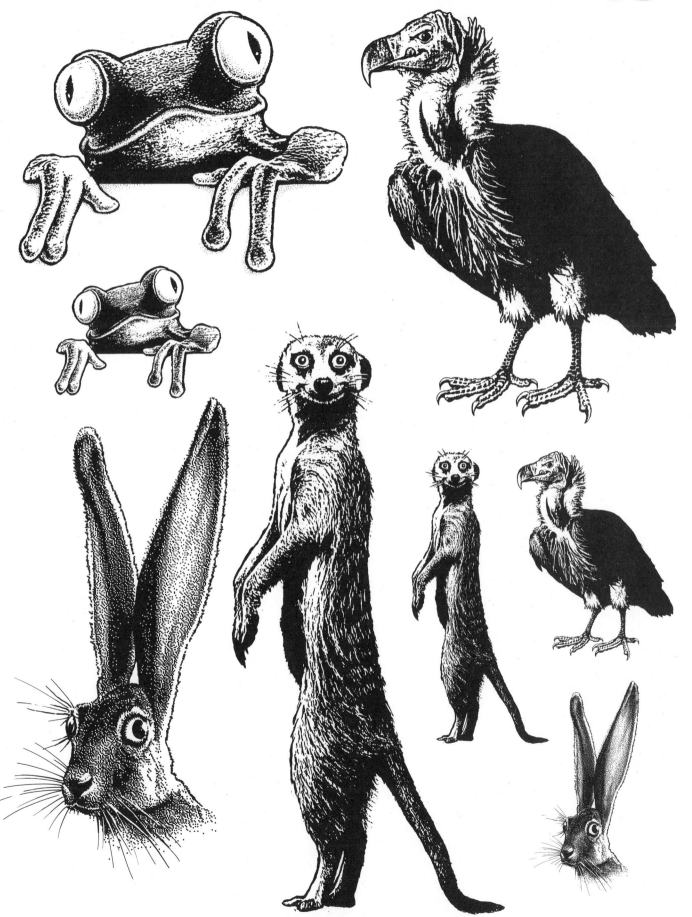

Something WILD

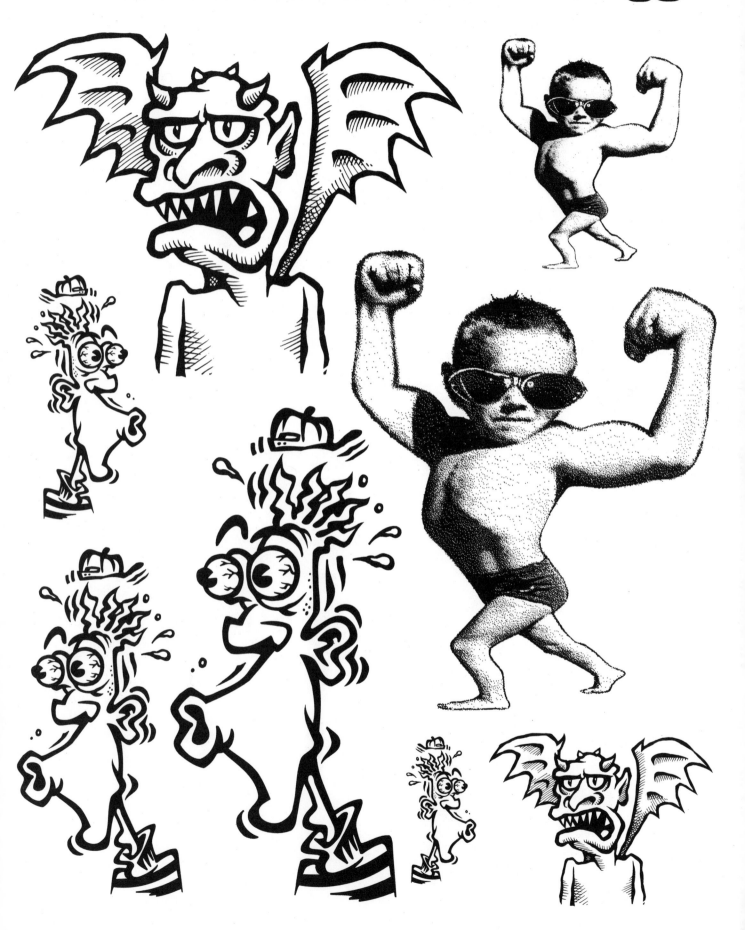

YOU BE THE JUDGE

Dance to the Beat

of a Different Drum.

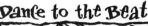

YOU BE THE JUDGE

Dance to the Beat

of a Different Drum.

CRITICS

CORNER

CRITICS

CORNER

KILLER EVENTZ

Mall *RAT* invasion

Mall *RAT* invasion

INDEX TO ARTSOURCE VOL.8

Youth Specialties Titles

Professional Resources

Developing Spiritual Growth in Junior High Students
Developing Student Leaders
Equipped to Serve: Volunteer Youth Worker Training Course
Help! I'm a Junior High Youth Worker!
Help! I'm a Sunday School Teacher!
Help! I'm a Volunteer Youth Worker!
How to Expand Your Youth Ministry
How to Recruit and Train Volunteer Youth Workers
How to Speak to Youth...and Keep Them Awake at the Same Time
One Kid at a Time: Reaching Youth through Mentoring
Peer Counseling in Youth Groups
Advanced Peer Counseling in Youth Groups
A Youth Ministry Crash Course

Discussion Starter Resources

Get 'Em Talking
4th-6th Grade TalkSheets
High School TalkSheets
Junior High TalkSheets
High School TalkSheets: Psalms and Proverbs
Junior High TalkSheets: Psalms and Proverbs
More High School TalkSheets
More Junior High TalkSheets
Parent Ministry TalkSheets
What If...? 450 Thought-Provoking Questions
    to Get Teenagers Talking, Laughing, and Thinking
Would You Rather...? 465 Provocative Questions
    to Get Teenagers Talking

Ideas Library

Combos: 1-4, 5-8, 9-12, 13-16, 17-20, 21-24, 25-28, 29-32, 33-
    36, 37-40, 41-44, 45-48, 49-52, 53-56
Ideas Index

Youth Ministry Programming

Compassionate Kids: Practical Ways to Involve Your Students in
    Mission and Service
Creative Bible Lessons in John: Encounters with Jesus
Creative Bible Lessons in Romans: Faith on Fire!
Creative Bible Lessons on the Life of Christ
Creative Junior High Programs from A to Z, Vol. 1 (A-M)
Creative Programming Ideas for Junior High Ministry
Dramatic Pauses
Facing Your Future: Graduating Youth Group with a Faith That
    Lasts
Great Fundraising Ideas for Youth Groups
More Great Fundraising Ideas for Youth Groups

Great Retreats for Youth Groups
Greatest Skits on Earth
Greatest Skits on Earth, Vol. 2
Hot Illustrations for Youth Talks
More Hot Illustrations for Youth Talks
Kickstarters: 101 Ingenious Intros to Just about Any Bible Lesson
Memory Makers
Hot Talks
Incredible Questionnaires for Youth Ministry
Junior High Game Nights
More Junior High Game Nights
Play It! Great Games for Groups
Play It Again! More Great Games for Groups
Road Trip
Spontaneous Melodramas
Super Sketches for Youth Ministry
Teaching the Bible Creatively
Up Close and Personal: How to Build Community in Your Youth
    Group
Wild Truth Bible Lessons
Worship Services for Youth Groups

Clip Art

ArtSource Vol. 1—Fantastic Activities
ArtSource Vol. 2—Borders, Symbols, Holidays, and Attention Getters
ArtSource Vol. 3—Sports
ArtSource Vol. 4—Phrases and Verses
ArtSource Vol. 5—Amazing Oddities and Appalling Images
ArtSource Vol. 6—Spiritual Topics
ArtSource Vol. 7—Variety Pack
ArtSource Vol. 8—Stark Raving Clip Art
ArtSource CD-ROM (contains Vols. 1-7)

Video

Edge TV
The Heart of Youth Ministry: A Morning with Mike Yaconelli
Next Time I Fall in Love Video Curriculum
Promo Spots for Junior High Game Nights
Understanding Your Teenager Video Curriculum

Student Books

Grow For It Journal
Grow For It Journal through the Scriptures
Wild Truth Journal for Junior Highers

We want to serve you! Send us your ideas so that we can draw them for future books to assist you in your ministry.

Name _____

Church or Ministry _____

Address _____

City _____

State _____ Zip _____

Phone _____

BONK!

B R A I N S T O R M   F O R M

Here are some ideas I'd like to see in future books:

Food Fun:

Fundraisers:

Group Stuff:

Music:

Summer:

Winter:

Copy and send to : Church Art Works™ • 875 High Street NE • Salem, Oregon 97301 • (503) 370-9377 • FAX (503) 362-5231

Church Art Works™/One Way Out®

ONE WAY OUT® FONTS

he perfect complement to your ArtSource clip art. With One Way Out® computer typefaces, you can make the xt of your fliers, announcements, and handouts as dynamic as the art.

Here are some examples:

THE THEMES™ PROGRAM

ese T-shirts and sweatshirts are pre-designed around current ministry themes and hot catch phrases. They are an cellent choice for your group or special-event garment needs. They're only **$8.95*** each for 100% cotton heavyweight s with a **minimum order of 24.** There are **no additional costs.** The shirts are name-dropped on the front with ur own group name or event. We can also provide you with the artwork on paper or computer disk so you can use e art consistently on all related publications and promotions. Getting personalized ministry tees has *NEVER BEEN MPLER!* Designs are changed each year, so be sure to call or write for the latest selections.

* Price as of 12/96. XXL's $10.50. Prices and designs subject to change.

 For info Call: **(503) 370-9377** Fax: **(503) 362-5231**